Daddy
Issues

Titanya Verdun Johnson

DEDICATION

TO EVERYONE WHO EVER HAD AN ISSUE, BE HEALED & GO HEAL
OTHERS BY TESTIFYING THAT YOUR PAIN HAD PURPOSE,
SHOUT OUT TO SOPHIA RUFFIN WHO INSPIRIED ME COACHED ME
IN THIS PROCESS, LAKEISHION GANHS I LOVE YOU EVERY PRAYER
& THE FINAL PUSH THANK YOU SIS. RACHELE CINEUS GIRL DOWN
SINCE 6THGRADE MY EDITOR LOVE U. AND MY DAD DWAYNE VERDUN
I LOVE YOU AND BLESS YOU I BELIEVE IN YOU LAST BUT NOT
LEAST MY MOMMA – BERNICE KING THANK YOU FOR TELLING ME
I CAN BE AND DO ANYTHING I WANT.

ABOUT THE AUTHOR- TITANYA VERDUN- JOHNSON

I was molested age 8
I learned how to steal age 8
I was physical abused age 11
I tried to murder someone age 11
I began drinking age 11
I got sexually violated age 11
I found out my father was on drugs
I shot my 1st gun
I started selling drugs age 15
I placed in alternative HIGH SCHOOL
I got placed on probation
I went to program for youth NCNW
I worked in the program and had counseling
I got internship from school at wbls 107.5
I worked in Radio & TV age 15- 19
I got married age 18
I went out town sold crack to bail out my now husband
I went on several robberies - planned a few
I had 2 children by age 20
I tried to kill the person my husband had an affair with
I got locked up for grand larceny placed on probation
I became a ride or die chick jail visits age 19-25
I became a Boss in music industry managing studios
I threw the most memorable celebrity events in NYC
I stopped when husband came out of jail
I was fighter in my marriage (now abusive)
I was depressed and drank til i couldnt remember my pain
I became full of lust & bisexual & even a swinger
I suggested we move to Georgia
I cried out to God, no reply so i thought ...
I moved to Georgia with my kids & husband & his friend
I was still being abused,
I couldn't get a job
I was about to work at Stroker's the strip club
I was now in deep water my husband tried to murder me
I decided to kill him since God didn't help me
I was on the news

I had an abortion
I was now left to raise my 2 kids only
I moved on with a friend of ours who was always there
I had 2 children with the friend
I was selling dvds & cds & bootleg pocketbooks
I was selling weed
I got baptized age 33
I got a job
I began to hear God speak
I got blessed with a big house and i had 2 cars
I got injured on my Job hit- my head blacked out
I had memory loss
I began to go to church everyday - i had no job
I took classes in church - Masterlife (discipleship)
I had a supernatural experience I saw Jesus
I became a teacher in the church
I went to women thou art loosed - I got delivered
I heard God say pack and go
I had to obey and move out of sin
I got filled with the Holy ghost
I obeyed
I was homeless
I got divorced
I was favored got a place
I live holy
I fell once I go up
I fear God
I began preaching weekly for 2yrs +
I went to mission trip to Haiti preached
I testify now !
I am author I give God all the Glory!
I am a comeback kid and I'm coming for you!

Daddy Issues —Chapter1

Super hero

He was my superhero, my friend, my Daddy. My Daddy was funny, strong, and he was handsome. I was the little girl that would run and jump with a huge smile every time I saw him. See my dad didn't live with us, he and my mother were not married. My mother and I lived in a house with my grandparents and aunt. My father would come and visit us often, but before it got dark my grandfather would knock on the room door and say "ok its late, he gotta go, he don't live here". For a while, I lived a pretty sheltered life, similar to that of a Disney kid. I went to catholic school; I had the white picket

9

fence, a swing set, and a dog name Jody Thomas. I even

played the flute in the school band. It was almost like a

fairytale, until one day a promise was broken and abuse

took place. As I mentioned before my dad didn't live

with us so when he would come by it was the highlight

of our day. I was just a kid but I can still remember the

romance my parents shared, the googley eyes they

would make at each other. I remember being in

between them, they were so in love and I could feel the

warmth and happiness. To know that I was a result of

that love felt good, like I was the heartbeat that kept

their love alive. Somewhere around the age of 7 my Dad

promised that he would take me to Coney Island, an

amusement park located in Brooklyn, N.Y. where people

went to get a hotdog and play some games but he didn't

keep his promise. He didn't come back like he said he

would. He told me he was sorry but then did it again.

Now this may seem like a corny story to you but watch

how one open door leads to another, what am I talking

about disappointment I was now lied to by my hero I

was let down.

At age 8 I was molested by an older female cousin

the bathroom. I was told to keep it a secret and I did.

And by the age 12 I would have been sexual violated age

this time by a grown man. Family secrets wow, that was

hard to type but the truth sets us all free. So now the

door of perversion , lust has been open. I'm telling you

the things that happen so we can identify where the

behavior came from and we can shut the door.

To this day, as an adult, I still wish that promise my

Dad made was never broken. Why? Why say that

you're going to do something and then don't do it? It just doesn't make sense. If you can't do it, then don't say it. Why would you leave me waiting, hoping and believing in you to do what you said? Y'all this was the beginning of my daddy issues, if only you could feel my heart.

Have you ever believed in someone that let you down? Do you feel like you are owed something even now? Do you have a memory that needs healing? I know I did and I do. Let's get healed together

Father in the name of Jesus we ask you to help us Lord we give you our pain our hurt and ask you God to guide us in how to forgive them, Lord you know

_____-hurt me, we want to move forward in our lives and we want to forgive them father and let go

of past disappointments Today God we begin a process

of healing we call on you for you are great you forgave

me in all I did now show me how to be more like you.

No more excuses on why I can keep being mad I choose

to be heal and let this go today I chose forgiveness in

Jesus name amen.

See the reason we prayed right there is because

that scared little girl had to grow up, and when she did

she had bitterness, doubt in men and expected to be

disappointed. Her trust was broken, how could it be

fixed? Only through healing and that healing comes

through forgiveness and prayer.

Titanya Verdun Johnson

Daddy issues- Chapter 2

I'mma kill him (secrets)

Well it was the spring time, this I remember for sure because we were headed up to Roy Wilkins Park to apply for jobs with my friends' teacher. I wasn't old enough yet to get my working papers but I was surely very hopeful that I could lie on the application and maybe get a job. I was about 11 or 12 years old. So you can picture the scene; my mom and I shared a room in my grandparent's house and we had a dresser, a TV, big bed and a stool. We also had roaches what? Yes, so that meant no eating in the room, my mom was strict on that. So, on that day my best friend who lived across the street came by with her mom who was going to take us to apply for a job at the camp. I was too young; she was older than me so I went along to try anyway. They were downstairs talking to my nana and then my mom called, in the same moment my dad stopped by. He was upstairs and had eaten a piece of chicken. Why am I telling you this? Just listen, so I was on the phone, you know the old school cordless phone with the antenna you had to pull up, and she said "make sure you don't eat in that room ty" I said" I'm not but daddy had a piece of chicken". Now I wasn't gonna get in trouble for my daddy's chicken crumbs, she said" let me speak to him". At that point he was in the bathroom, when he came out I gave him the phone and then sat on my stool to pick out what top I was gonna wear so I could leave. All I heard was "I hate that little B@#$!" I looked up and I went flying back from a back hand slap off of the stool.

Yes you heard me he back slapped me so hard I flew outta my seat. I immediately jumped up and ran down stairs to get a knife crying and screaming my nana and my friend and her mom thought I was joking, I was dramatic at times, always being silly but this was real. I grabbed a knife flew back upstairs and then I couldn't find him he went back in the bathroom when he came out he went downstairs I tried to stab him while he was going down stairs but he moved so fast that I missed (thank God).

My grandmother then asked him "what's going on"? I hollered "I'm gonna kill him". She took the knife away and he left, then she sat me down and patched my swollen bloody lip and face up. My Nana then told me "now we gonna say you fell down the stairs cause if you tell your grandfather or your uncles they will kill him". I thought to myself, that's what I want and then she reiterated "now don't you tell anyone". We called my mom and told her.

I didn't see my dad for a while after that, I hated him and I wanted my mom to hate him for hurting her baby. I wasn't cool with lying to my grandpa because he loved me and was very protective over me. This is when the doors for secrets and lies had began to open wider, not only that I now felt unprotected. I felt like where's the was the justice? Who was actually defending me?

When I finally did see my dad he was forced by my Mom to apologize. I was crushed at the fact that she continued to love someone who hurt me. This y'all are daddy issues, but wait what about God didn't he give me these parents? So at this point I'm not feeling him

either, yes I'm talking about God. I'm feeling like why

me? What did I do to deserve this? Have you ever held

on to a secret and lied? Have you ever felt like someone,

or even God should have protected you? Well so have I,

let's heal today:

Father in the name of Jesus I ask for forgiveness for

telling lies and keeping secrets. Help me lord to

understand that it wasn't my fault, and I ask that you

forgive me father for blaming you, and hardening my

heart toward you and harboring un-forgiveness in my

heart for those that have offended me. God I pray for

every child right now lord, that may be abused or

harmed emotionally, physically and mentally. I pray

that they find Peace, and that you protect them with the psalms 91 hedge of protection, I thank you Lord that this is now a testimony, I am still standing , and I am able to forgive and ask you to forgive them father; for they know not what they do. Lord help me even with the words that feel the tight in my chest even as I pray, I release it all to you, anger, rage, revenge. In the mighty name of Jesus, I give this over to you Lord. I choose to forgive, and I am protected by the father. Amen.

See, now the reason we prayed right there is because this little girl now had anger, rage; a spirit of violence had entered. There was definitely something wrong with my response being to kill my father. I now desired to have a man; a husband that I could be sure would protect me. Even though I was trying to protect me, it didn't make it right. I don't care what the law says I now go by the word of God. If someone hits you, he said give them the other cheek to hit you again, not go get a knife. Glory to God, I'm here and I am forgiven, and I forgave, have you? Come on let's get right! Don't turn the page if you still need to forgive. I give you permission to refund this book if you're going to stay stuck. Don't go any further until you say the name, situation, and tell anger, revenge, hate all of those wack unclean spirits they have to go now! In the name of Jesus, up and out now! You good now? Good.

Titanya Verdun Johnson

Daddy issues Chapter 3 -

NOT THE FATHER

Ok, so now I'm feeling some type of way that no one protected me and really my dad was supposed to be my super hero remember? Now I am disappointed and I began to lie. I went from being a catholic school good girl who got the honor roll all the time to a secret keeping, angry person who now had unforgiveness. Man the devil don't play fair, I was young an violated. Although I appeared smiley and happy I was broken , I learned how to disguise my pain. I went to a public middle school located in Hollis, Queens in New York. My father would ride his bike up to the school with a pouch on his waist full of lotto tickets and ask people did had they seen me while showing them a picture of me that he carried in his wallet. How embarrassing, why is it embarrassing you ask? Because now something was wrong. I couldn't figure it out but something strange was going on with my dad, so I began to tell people that he was my step dad and that my real father died in a war. What war? I didn't know, but I knew I wasn't claiming him.

My mother decided to moved out of my grandparent's house and get a place for me, her and my dad. I was the only child between them two I had an older brother through my father, from a previous relationship, who he highlighted so much that it made me jealous I wasn't a boy. So now I was thinking maybe my dad don't like me cause I'm not a boy, I wanted to dress like a boy. I really wanted a fathers love and protection, but since I now experience rejection that door was now wide open rejection. I lost my identity and was drowning in pain. I began drinking at 11. In addition to everything else, my mother was now moving me away from my safe zone my Grandparents. I had hate in my heart toward my Dad and we were suppose to live together? The real question was why does God hate me so much that this is my life? How was this supposed to work? I decided if he ever tried to put his hands on me again I was gonna cut him, I traveled with a box cutter; I even knew how to hide it in my mouth and flip it with my tongue. May I say something? That is dumb. Can't you imagine if it would have cut my tongue? Jesus, the stupid things I did. Ok so now I became sort of rebellious or at least I wasn't listening to him. I didn't honor him; he was no longer my hero. Later I would discover some news that would break my heart even further. I had friends that hung out on the park benches and sold drugs that had been friends of mine since forever! I would kick it with them while they would sell to the neighborhood feens. One day I was sitting in the alley with my homeboy and some others keep in mind, the only people that came into this alley were people who were buying drugs. My homeboy was like "Tanya lets go get some Chinese food, let's go to the store and lets go this way", I said" nah I'm good we just ate". He seemed real bossy about me going to the store or at least leaving the area. I then realized that it was because my father, my X-super hero, was riding down this alley and my friend didn't want me to know HE was buying drugs. At that moment I hardened up and said "I don't care", and when my father saw me he said "Tanya what you doing over here"? I said "wow you could at least buy from me, keep it in the family", and he ignored me. I was furious, was I selling drugs at that time? No, I didn't even litter, remember I was the Disney kid, but all these events that were taking place made me feel like reality was whooping my butt. My father, a crackhead? Really God? Now I'm pissed I hate drugs so much, now I want to sell them; and so it began. It wasn't hard and the drug addicts were nice, they were people's aunts and uncles. It was only when they tried to get drugs on credit you would have a problem cause they wouldn't pay you back. Where did I get drugs from? Well when you live in New york its not that hard , and I bought it from my homeboy, he would re-up for me. Now I'm furious cause' my mother moved us out of the house of

safety and she's with him, and he's got issues for real!

On the day I decided to tell her about him was the day

he stole my jewelry, and my drugs and we had a fight.

Let me back up. He had said something slick to me while

I was ironing my clothes and threaten to slap me again

and I put the hot iron so close to his face and said "your

life was spared 1 time but no one can protect you now, I

will murder you"! He left out of my room and never

again in my life did I have to worry about him

threatening me with his hands. I protected me. Now

Pride rose up and I cant explain how good I felt not

letting me down.

When I left for school that day and returned

home he had gone through my closet taken my drugs

and my jewelry box was upside down and empty, my collection of watches was missing. He claimed a fight took place with his brother and some friend in our home. That's why things were out of place all of my watches gone all my jewelry gone. This is serious guys, My dad needed help.

I began to see a decline in my mother's happiness, she worked 9-5 came home, cooked, and repeated that cycle again and again. On the day I was prepared to tell her about him being on drugs , My friend was over my house, we were in my room talking and he opens door and started talking to my friend while interrupting me, didn't even speak to me; I asked him to exit the room but he continued. I asked him if he could please leave us, but then he went and told my mom something and she came back telling me I had to respect my father. I began to tell her how I felt about him and she slapped me, I'm sure I yelled and was crunk because I felt like how can you defend him when you didn't even defend me, and now you slap me and all I could see was him in the background, it was like him vs me and so I responded, and it wasn't pretty. I can't believe I raised my hands on my mother, how did things get so turned around? I hated that everything was falling apart and didn't understand I didn't even know the all those open doors now lead to frustration rebellion, I never knew the devil could be blamed for this type of stuff then. I was heartbroken because I loved my mom, even though I was tight that she didn't defend me. Now she defended him. Dude like at least be neutral, don't pick sides. As a result, I got offended and wounded again and now the rebel is arising I want to run away. I hated them, and I began to look for acceptance and comfort and I found it in liquor. I would drink to hide my pain, I would write raps, also another form of expression, here's one I remember clearly, at that age –

I didn't ask to be here, So who do I ask to go? I wish I was never born on the real though, My thoughts are steadily flowing Thinking of away to escape, Because this is the type of life I love to hate.

So now I felt rejected, lonely, and a host of other things, and I couldn't understand why me? What did I do to deserve a family like this? I was now selling drugs, lying about who my father was, being rebellious and drinking. I ran away for several days, stayed at a friends' house, eventually I ended up back at my grandparents' house; which was across the street and down the block from my mother and father. My mother took me to court and sought help for me through the judge. She had me registered for PINs (Person In Need of Supervision).I was placed on a probation. I then went to counseling and some programs that blessed my life. So shout out to that! I actually got my first job through them the NCNW (national council of Negro women). The program name was youth readiness. They did something that hadn't been done before, they showed me, ME. What am I saying? They had a video camera and they asked me questions about myself. They said, "Tell me a little about yourself", one week later they played the tape back to me and it was in that moment that I realized I was more, I was greater then that broken girl slouching in a chair; referring to herself as a Leo who lives in Queens, New York. Surely there had to be more to me than that! This program helped me discover my identity, at least a piece of my identity. When I saw how I looked, I asked myself, how does the world to see me? I had given up on happiness, love and promises. I was broken and bitter at a young age. I felt dirty and didn't even consider God cause he was in control I in fact blamed him for my pain, My heart was harden and I didn't even no it.

I learned how to mask it very well. I wanted to hurt those who hurt me, and I truly believed that there was logic to that. If I hurt you, it was because you hurt me. It was my job to make you understand that hurting isn't nice and you would stop hurting me or anyone else. The point of revenge was to teach a lesson that we shouldn't hurt others. Now wait a minute, this made no sense. In reality, only hurt people, HURT people. If you want a different result, you must do a different thing.

Stabbing the person that stabs you does not solve the

problem; it SPREADS THE PAIN.

Let us pray:

Father, in the name of Jesus, I want to say thank you Lord. Thank you for loving me. Thank you for forgiving me. Thank you for blessing me, and thank you for strength. Lord we just talked about a whole lot and it stirred up a lot of unpleasant memories. I ask that what ever pain or memory that is being stirred up in the person reading this book, be comforted by you. I ask you to supernaturally provide peace and light to any dark situation in their lives. I pray right now for every parent who has a child that is hurting. I ask for

healing Lord, mend the broken hearts. I come against the spirit of suicide right now, in the name of Jesus! I decree and declare that every runaway is running back home. I pray right now for those who had an addiction to anything, we break the power of the addiction right now, and we call those people passionate, hungry, and thirsty for righteousness, for your word and for your will. My prayer is that you will receive the love of God so that the root of bitterness will be uprooted and that forgiveness will be what you are clothed in. I break the spirit of entitlement , I pray for unity in families. I pray for restoration and reconciliation in Jesus name, Amen.

See now the reason we prayed was this little girl was growing up and she had bitterness, and felt which doesn't just go away. She felt like the world owed her.

Although I didn't want to be hard, I felt I had no choice,

so we prayed today to show there's always a choice, and

we choose life, we choose the healing.

Daddy Issues Chapter 4 –

Now what – High school days

I was now working my job at the NCNW, I was on youth probation and in counseling. I found the youth program helpful, they gave attention to areas of my life that seemed like no one cared about. While I was working with them I felt loved and understood. I was living with my grandparents and I was enjoying life. I was going to August Martin High School so many cuties (cute boys). I spotted one that was observed in a relationship and I thought wow I want that exactly how he treats her I want that. In fact I wanted it so bad I took it, what does that mean I learned at an early age how to get what I wanted him and they broke up and he was mine. I now had a boyfriend and my family knew him he came over for holidays. He was cute his birthday was the day after mine, and I thought we would be together forever! That was a lie, after 2 and ½ years that relationship ended and I thought I was really broken again. I just didn't like the idea of having a relationship then losing it. So it appears everything is disappointing me.

With music having an huge influence on my life I lived Hip-Hop in the 90's we had walk man and listen to mix tapes, I still dressed like a boy but I was cute though and had good hair, this is before everybody could by good hair when things where real. In fact I was teased and called mixed breed and most of the dudes that tried to holler at me was because my hair. Ok so the music I listen to and loved had lyrics mostly about Sex and being someone's secret, keep it on the down low, gotta get a ruffneck etc. I repeated lyrics of songs but I ended up living out ever lyric. I had no clue then the power of my words, I had no clue who I was music was my drug and it filled me up I needed Hip-hop you don't understand it was my escape I imagined videos to songs and got upset when the real video came out and it wasn't like the one I created in my head. whatever you feed will grow I was feeding the lust, pain and secrets.

Now its high school days I have settled with the fact that my dad has a problem drinking and drugging but I am denying he is really my father. I was ashamed of him. I couldn't understand how I was supposed to love him; he hurt me, and my mother. He couldn't be trusted. I watched my super hero fail, at least that's what it felt like and now since I saw a process from Good to bad I now equated that to everyone. What I mean is I thought anyone could fail me, so I trusted no one. I blamed God for my pain I felt fatherless, wounded by pain, rejection and disappointment.

In my mind I created the idea that growing into women hood that I needed someone to protect me. I built up invisible walls and didn't see my self as having protection from my Father I still desired a Father. I now looked to fill that empty space with relationship with my boyfriend. I had imaginations of the perfect love and once my relationship crumbled their goes that! Now God let me down, my Father let me down and now my boyfriend for 2.5 years- that's long when u in High

School.

I decided to plan my future I would have 3 husbands when I grew up, I was now planning for failure do you see that. I was bitter not just toward my Dad, but men in general. This thought process affected my outlook on what my future would be like. I was actually blaming God for what I did and didn't get from my father. All these relationships are connected we will connect the dots later on.

God revealed to me that every judgment I placed on my Dad, could easily be me. I came from him judging him was me judging me. At times I was just like him. I became a thief a liar a fast talker. It could be me under the influence of something. Instead of Judging him I was designed to be his intercessor the person who prays for him and covers him.

I can't explain it; it was a conversation in my head and I supernaturally started to feel compassion towards him. All of those years of hating him had stopped. I wasn't going to a church t his was just an experience God gave me. One day I hated him with a passion, and the next I wished I could help him. The power of God is real, even when I was living lost God spoke to me and touched my heart. I had a revelation an understanding that my Dad was sick and needed help. Thank you Lord.

Let's Pray

Father in the name of Jesus we thank you God for being loving kind and awesome, thank you for loving us no matter the things we have done thank you for forgiving us, Now God I ask you to teach us how to LOVE like you

and keep no record of wrong doing. I pray today that

anyone who has a problem a issue with their Father

family/friend I pray they would begin to feel

compassionate and would now let go of bitterness

rejection , pain the entitlement and un-forgiveness.

God allow this moment to be a divine moment of

supernatural exchange pain for prayers. Lord turn the

hearts of the Fathers touch the hearts of the children,

Lord let forgiveness rain on families today Get the

Glory out of every dark situation in our life Lord. We

insert your word for peace in our families, let the weak

say I am strong the poor say I am rich. God we love

you. Give us a revelation and Father we ask for wisdom

in all that we do, lord I pray for restoration and

reconciliation in Jesus name amen.

Titanya Verdun Johnson

Daddy Issues Chapter 5

Married at age 18- THUG LIFE

Ok, so now my qualifications were you had to be an ex-thug wanting more for your self. Why did I want a thug? Because to me that meant he wasn't a punk and that if I had a problem then he could handle it. It also meant that he wouldn't get older and try to live a life style of the youth. I knew even then I was destined for greatness. I didn't want a weak or wack partner. Again, as a result of my daddy issues I wanted a superhero from the hood y'all. I had been rejected, abused, and ignored by my natural father. I wanted now to be accepted, loved and affirmed. I wanted the attention I never got as a little girl. As far as it goes with me and God I felt like I was outta of the go to heaven loop according to me being a sinner who felt like I couldn't stop, What I learned in Catholic school I thought I was never gonna see God, I keep messing up, so me and God had no relationship. I was looking for a man to call daddy. I had a grandfather who showed me love; however I wanted to know why I wasn't accepted by my dad.

See I began to believe that no man could be honest or faithful so I decided I was always gonna have a plan B. I decided in my mind there was no one man that could be real enough for me. I gave up on love and had a friend for every day of the week. I was upset with men and how they treated women. I had friends that were heart broken and I decided that wasn't gonna be me. I would treat men how they treated women, I thought it was cool to be a female playa that wasn't giving it up, not yet, or to everybody yet at least. I valued my self and the only reason I wasn't a virgin is because I was sexually violated at a young age, and that violation opened the door and I had was controlled at a young age by the spirit of perversion. That's another testimony for another book so stay tuned for that; but yes, violated by both male and female. This opened the door for perversion and lust. I now had a sexual appetite that demanded satisfaction, so much so that I had an addiction to masturbation and porn.

Moving on I had daddy issues y'all underneath the surface. At the age of 18 still broken from daddy issues, I ended up meeting a 19 year old male who had a tough life and had expressed a desire to change. He was in

college, played ball and was to me a cleaned up thug!

For me he was just a day of the week I went on dates

throughout the week and was honest with each male,

that we were all just friends. I would tease them and say

"it's not like y'all want to get married". I figured if I

made all of them wait, some of them would fall off

eventually. I loved being free! Then something

happened, most of the guys began to fall off but one

remained persistent. He was going through a personal

issue and that caused us to become even closer. Within

he proposed I said "yes" thinking I was gonna be rocking

a ring forever. Who in the hood gets married I really

thought he just did the proposal to clear all the others

out the way.

I later figured out that it was a snare. Why do I call it a snare? Because it took me off course of my destiny, but God placed me right back on track. It has been revealed to me that I fell in a snare and I asked God where the way of escape was. Why let me fall in the snare? He said "I provided you a way of escape" I said "when"? I was immediately reminded of the week before I got married, he asked my mother what she thought about us getting married, she said "I think young people should wait"! We were married the next week. Had I done what Ephesians chapter 6 says, "Children obey your parents" the outcome would have been different. God said to me that if I would have just waited then the one I married would have been locked up and I wouldn't have gone through being a prison wife, raising 2 kids, making visits to upstate prisons. I blamed God for my disobedience. You can't get married to make sex legal, I was broken and I needed healing. I needed healing before I could become a wife I was a broken little girl. Now married at 18 this man is my world where everything else has failed me I just knew he wont we had a promise together.

Before the 3rd year of the marriage he had cheated and I took the vows serious til death do us apart,. So I attempted to kill what was taking us apart the girl he cheated with, see the spirit of murder was ready to be activated I went door to door with a 380 gun in my nine west pocketbook while pregnant. Some of you may say that's crazy, well I made it make good sense to me. I had already did a year in prison with him, been out of town sold drugs for bail money, the good girl had gone bad or was she ever good? That too is another

story for another book. I thank God that he had another

plan for my life.

Dealing with how to forgive after being

cheated on was difficult. I couldn't understand why that

happened. Soul ties are real , when you sleep with

someone you connect with them, I felt every time the 2

of them where together. Even when I tried to forget it I

couldn't I thought why was I not enough. so to avoid any

more cheating we opened the marriage up. What does

that mean we would have no secrets, I mean from

threesomes to swinger events I refused to be hurt that

way again. Now was this what I really wanted no I rather

a husband that wouldn't cheat, but I tried to be smart

and say if the fun is in sneaking now there's no need to

sneak.

I wanted protection but what I got 10 years later in this same marriage was a cheating spouse, body blows, and patches of hair pulled out. I was knocked out at times, fights like the UFC I'm not joking, ask about me. We even made it to the news in the year 2008/2009 when my children and I were held hostage in our home, at gunpoint and he tried to take my life. Don't get it twisted I had made a decision to end his life. I remember clearly complaining to God and saying I don't wanna go to jail and be gay. I won't be able to eat Lobster and baked potatoes, this wasn't fair. I remember a loud thunder sound in my ears and God said "I'm not letting you go to jail". I actually heard the voice of God. I thought to myself that can't be God because God would know if you do what I'm about to do you go to jail.

Besides, I thought where was God when my butt was

getting whooped. Truth was I couldn't t believe that I

had to now protect myself again, now I felt dissed by

God again. First I was dissed because the father he gave

me, now I'm married and this is failing. I gave all, did all,

Why God? Why? Well there's so much more I could

share and will in time. I am a survivor, what doesn't kill

you, really makes you stronger if you get healed. You can

become bitter after you invest time, love, money plus

kids in a person. I flipped on God like "yo I thought you

liked marriage? You played me". God said "what I put

together let no man tear it apart, I didn't put y'all

together" . I was like why can I hear God so clear now?

Let us Pray:

Father in the name of Jesus, we say thank you Lord for your will, your way. Thank you for the plan that you have for us to prosper and not harm us. The plan to give hope and a future. I pray God for everyone lord, that may be in a violent relationship. I ask you to give them strength and wisdom to get to the hope and the future. I ask Lord that you break off all fear and give them courage and provide a way of escape. I pray psalms 91 hedge of protection over them and I thank you for aligning them with their destinies. Today God I ask that marriages be done according to who you picked, not who we're feeling but who you have chosen and designed for us. I pray for any relationships that are not under your covenant today. I pray you remove the barrier, whatever is hindering that man/woman from committing in holy matrimony. I break that barrier now in the name of Jesus and I call forth holy alliances. I speak purity to those reading this that you have called. I thank you that they will hunger and thirst after righteousness. I pray for every marriage in Jail. I lift up the relationship with you God that is so important. I love you and thank you for supernaturally healing those that are reading this. In Jesus name Amen

Daddy Issues Chapter 6

Me on the search for the real

Fast forward, now I'm New York girl living in Georgia. My husband is locked up and I have daddy issues for real now! I never wanna love again. I never wanted my children to deal with a step dad and then he leaves them, so I began to try to avoid disappointment for my kids by not allowing any one in. I figured that if I was gonna marry again it would have to be someone I knew all my life, and guys this story I couldn't make up, your girl lady ty Titanya connected with, mated with, had children with and started a whole new family with my husband's best friend; who was also my friend. Jaw dropping right?! As grimey as it may seem, I didn't do it for any reason other than that, he was there for me when no one else was. His wife left him, my man tried to kill me, and now we're both in Georgia; so we made lemonade out of our lemons. Two more kids later yes, I now have 4 kids (2 with the 1st man and 2 with the 2nd man) but, he was my friend so surely this would work ha! No, God spoke again! Wait a minute Jesus, why you weren't you talking before I did the act? Don't talk now, 2 kids a whole house and 2 cars later. One day at church, I decided to get baptized, we randomly went to church. And I began to hear God more, I was still turning up but something changed. The Lord said" I need you to pack do an Abraham walk this is not what I have for you". I didn't know the books of the bible, let alone the stories in it, so I read about Abraham. All I knew of the word were things I discovered through my own revelations, and God showing me through my real life situations.

Having said that, again the Lord said "Ty this is not what

I have for you, you settled you don't even like him, this

was convenient" What? This cant be God talking that's

what I'm saying. So I search for what was real, I joined a

church and I started sitting in the corner but, before long

God had his way and 4 years later I was front and center.

I served in prison ministry, tithers' campaign, and

children's ministry. I taught classes, I did school of

biblical studies, and discipleship groups. I began a

relationship with church but still needed one with Christ.

One day I went to a "Woman Thou Art Loosed" event, a

conference held by Bishop TD Jakes, and my life was

forever changed something happen at that event that I

never believed could happen. It was a 3 day event,

When I got there the first day people were speaking in

tongues and it sounded crazy to me, because I didn't understand anything about the holy ghost. There was a point when the bishop stretched his hand towards the gospel singer and she fell out. I thought to myself wait, what happened? Is she gonna get back up? This is crazy, why would she fall? My thoughts were, let me get out of here. It was near the end and I was confused. The bishop began to walk the floor and people were running up to him and falling out, I thought that was dumb why go up to someone and fall out? I proceeded to leave the event he walked by me and then turned around and he said "I have been praying for you", and I thought yeah right, but ok. He looked directly in my eyes and said it again, "I'm praying for you, and I have been praying for you". I thought ok why is he stopping here with me when all these people trying to get to him, and then his hand reached toward me and I remember looking down at myself and saying, how am I seeing me? I out of my body or in the spirit realm of things, I saw the entire arena I was leaned back like the matrix and I was screaming for a very long time and I questioned how I was able to scream, if I didn't have any breath left to scream.? And I heard a voice say "my daughter even in the spirit you gonna question me"? I said "who is that? Oh my that's God, am I dead"? Then God said "you're not screaming I'm getting something out of you". I asked "what's in me? I'm nice, I feed the homeless. The lord said "bitterness, resentment, hate, anger and a list of things". All of a sudden the scream no longer sounded like me it sounded like screeching sounds, unclean spirits. I returned to my body and I was delivered. I went home and the Lord told me to stop all forms of physical activity sex y'all, he said stop having it, I was like God how is that gonna work? Nonetheless, I obeyed and 2 months after the conference I did a faith walk and moved out of my house of sin into the promise of God. My children and I were without a home. We stayed in 1 room, all 4 of us. God was faithful and blessed me with my own 5 months later. I moved in this house with nothing but faith. When I moved out I left everything, all the furniture, everything! Now I had a home, I was like God umm what we gonna do? He blessed me, furnished everything I mean God gave me more than I had with any man I had ever been with. Within 1-2 months I had brand new couches, washer/dryer, 2 dining room tables, 2 sets of bunk beds; I mean everything and more! Thank you Jesus! I walked away from the life I knew, I obeyed God and he gave me double.

I finally found the REAL. My home is his home. God dwells here everything is dedicated to him. This house is holy, I wasn't raised with the word of God all over the place, but I know one thing its not hurting us its blessing my kids. The battle we fight is spiritual and the word of God is the only thing that can cut up any situation, try it, and apply it. I'm a witness, instead of cursing someone out say this; greater is he that is in me than he that is in this world. Demons tremble at the word. If someone's acting mean, that's not heavenly, apply the word. I began to hear from God so much to the point he would share with me things he didn't agree with, God began to tell me things to tell others, I was fasting and praying and getting to know this father in God that I hadn't known ever.

Let us pray:

Father in the name of Jesus I pray for the person reading this to be stretched to the next level in you God. Next level in faith I pray that they will make you smile God, that when they hear your instruction they will obey. I pray that they get a revelation from you God for their prayer life.

I pray for their fasting, relationship with you, and I pray for their process. God anything that may have come up to block the relationship with you, we ask that it be removed now in the name of Jesus. We ask that you expose any wolves in sheep's clothing and hidden agendas. Father I pray that they would have an experience with you in there homes even as they read this; that you would deliver them right now lord from those things that they don't even know are there. You did it for me lord and I'm asking you to do it for them. Deliver them; set them free Lord, any unclean spirit hidden in your life I command it to go now in the name of Jesus. I apply the blood of Jesus to your life, to your body right now in the name of Jesus! Receive it. You are being delivered right now! Thank you Lord for the promise over their life remember your promise to them and I decree and declare the promises of God are yes and amen so let them live out the promises of Peace that surpasses all understanding. Supply all their needs God according to your riches and your glory. Lord today we break old cycles, generational curses right now in the name of Jesus. Thank you lord for making all things new! Heal their heart tonight God and we speak to the trauma right now in the mind, in the heart, and

in the GI tract; in every hidden part, we command it to go now in Jesus name Amen.

The reason we had to pray is because you need to know that at the age 33 God made me brand new, like I know that's a scripture but it came to life he walked me through everything, and he told me he pulled me out of the fire so I could go back and pull others out so this is why your reading my business because I am anointed. I have been crushed for the glory of God that means I'm still here even after all of that to tell you there will be glory after this. That you can make it, keep pressing on. I feel lighter already. When God touches you, you can't be untouched. Here I am 5 years later living a holy lifestyle of peace and joy. It is possible!

Daddy Issues Chapter 7

My Father and I Daddies Little Girl

Ok y'all, like we went from a little girl to a grown woman really fast. After disappointment, hurt divorce and seeking God. In the midst of me asking questions the Lord began to reply to me. I started hearing from God like some hear from their best friend. He gives me instructions daily and every time I follow what he says I am blessed, like the things he says doesn't make sense to my natural mind, you need the mind of faith. Here I am living this holy lifestyle, I have no friends, I live in church and my appetite is different; like I can't do the things I use to. I have decide to follow this Jesus that came to see about me, this relationship is so personal

I was healed by a God, I had given up on. Wow! He could have said forget you Ty, but he didn't.

One day I was chillin and the lord said "you never loved anybody "I said "who you talking to"? Like surely I have and began to list 3 people. The Lord said "no they were only filling in the blanks, you love lobster, the date, the movies, whatever vacation but the person didn't really matter as long as they were doing what you wanted". The lord said "you can't love anybody until you experience the Love of the father". I thought well what's taking so long? God revealed to me that I was hurt and broken, my heart was hardened. He showed me that every relationship I had I tried to fill the void of who my father wasn't, with a mate. God said" Ty you wanted a protector only cause you got hurt". In regards to my next relationship he said "you wanted a simple lovable guy with no kids because you knew he would be there for his kids unlike the first one who was locked up".

God revealed that I had motives in my relationships. Even when it looked good I didn't even care about who they were. How do I know because the Lord asked me something about each mate and I couldn't answer, and he said see they served a purpose to you and once that wasn't being fulfilled you dropped them or no longer wanted to be with them that's not love then I read 1 Corinthians 13 Love is patient, Love is kind, it doesn't boast it does not envy it doesn't keep a record of wrong doing.

God told me if I loved any of them I would still love them, I was like "huh god"? He said just like you lost a close friend and you mourn and cry the ending of these relationships should be mourning and crying if you loved them. I asked why and he explained "you never give up Ty it's like how I love you, you couldn't have loved them because you haven't experienced it unfailing". That day I discovered I had a hard heart toward God, I had what they call the orphan spirit, I felt like an outcast, like why me? I took it though; I thought that pain was mine to carry.

God wanted to heal my heart, he wanted me to experience him as a good father, so after he told me so politely that I was selfish and had a selfish love that had nothing to do with loving others, but everything to do with what I needed from them. I thought WOW God is awesome! To know all about me, to love me when I'm mean. I received healing that day I felt the love of the father I had been going to church and conferences wanting to fit in, wanting to belong but you know what you must know who you are in him before trying to belong anywhere else. I belong to God and in the search for my TRUE identity; I had to accept that I am a daughter, no more orphan heart. I belong, and when that happened I was able to see so much more clearly about what I was called to do. I understood it all as a testimony no more pain, and blame in God, true freedom. I don't just wear a cross I understand I bear a cross, living a lifestyle of denying my flesh daily.

The point in this entire book is one relationship effects them all, what am I saying. Your relationship with God matters, and if you don't have one this could be the reason everything around you not stable. Matthew 6:33 seek ye first the kingdom of God and his righteousness and all these things will be added unto you. " when your relationship with the creator gets aligned everything else will fall into place. I was broken, and I was angry at God and blamed him for what my natural father did I blamed God for allowing me to go threw what I went threw, I had no clue that what I was going threw was gonna give me a testimony and I was being crushed in areas because I was anointed to go back in the fire and get others who feel stuck unworthy those who have learned how to mask their depression.

In order to produce olive oil there must be a process. The olive tree must be planted and grown and produce olives, then the tree must be shaken the olive beaten and crushed and processed squeezed and then there comes and oil. Does this sound like your life I don't care If you're a male or a female young or old? If you just hold on don't give up if it didn't kill you I'm here to tell you it made you stronger.

The anointing breaks yokes it destroys what was holding you. It breaks cycles the anointing the reason you were crushed beaten and you survived cause you are anointed! You are a survivor you now can go and free others (in Jesus name) of the very thing that tried to kill you you know have power and authority!

Let us pray:

Father I ask that you fill every empty space with your love and drive out all things that's not like you. Teach us how to love today lord, reveal to the person reading

these words, the areas you want to heal and make new. Surrender is the word, we surrender, say this: I surrender to you every area of my life! it is now under the submission of Jesus Christ I apply the blood of Jesus to every memory and ask you Lord to make all things new, seal it with the holy spirit in Jesus name amen.

The reason we prayed is because that's how we kick it with GOD, now I charge you with a praise! This is the best part of the book you actually gotta get up and give God the glory! surely as its seven chapters you can shout 7 times. Jump, clap, something! Come on praise' em he has been better than Good to me and you. We made it, and now we're going back in the fire to get others anointed and appointed. This scripture is why I live revelation 12:11 they overcame by the blood of the lamb and the word of there testimonies. Lets break it down the keys to overcoming is this, the blood of the lamb which is what? Jesus. Very good now I need you to say it again out loud "AND" – the word of their (that's you) testimonies, this is how we overcome by Jesus and our testimonies.

This means you must speak, you must not be ashamed, and you must come forth. You represent the Almighty (and) God has already added you in the book. You are the generation of AND, I like to say I look forward to reading your book Mr. / Ms. AND. God bless you it's been real folks waiting on you!

THANK YOU !

Your time is important and I thank you for investing your

time in reading my book I pray it blessed you. I

appreciate you.

I was encouraged and pushed by Sophia Ruffin. I knew

her for 9 months exactly and I now give birth today to

my book, this is dope.

Other Books :

"Holy who? Yes You"! you can live a life of Holiness

Prayers in the Hood.

How to love what you hate!

The devil in the pulpit

Stay connected:

ladytythegreat.com

Finally Shout out to you ! I pray this book blessed you. I want to encourage you, You are Great greatness lives in you I pray today if you don't already have Jesus Christ as your personal Lord and savoir – I pray today is a day that you settle your daddy issues and you surrender to God. Even if you don't know how or you think your not ready, If you want Peace, joy, deliverance its all available. All you have to do is invite him in. Say this Lord reveal your self to me I want to know more of you, I give you my whole heart have your way I surrender show me your plan for me, be the Lord of my life lead me guide me protect me. In Jesus name Amen

I pray you are healed and that you will allow God to operate on your heart. In me telling my testimony it was done so you too can over come. if God can use me surely he can use you be healed and in Jesus name you are not rejected you are loved by God . I release the Love of the Father over and in you, perfect love drives out all fear! You are better already. I believe!

If you agree say amen!

Be healed

Be Great

and

Testify!

I pray this book has encouraged you to forgive love and reconcile with our Heavenly Father and or-

- Father/ Step Father

- Husband / X- husband

- Uncle /Cousin

- Child /Son

- Anyone you hurt /who hurt you (Offense)

- Anyone you had an issue with

List names of People you forgive!

Yes write it! Release it!

_____

_____

Scriptures that helped me in my process

JER 29:11 "For I know the plans I have for you thus says the Lord plans to prosper you not plans to harm you plans to give you hope and a future " –

Ok so for me if your in a harmful situation that's not Gods plan you gotta press out of anything that is less then prospering you!

Isaiah 54:17 No weapon formed against you shall prosper, and every tongue which rises against you in judgment You shall condemn. This is the heritage of the servants of the Lord, and their righteousness is from Me," says the Lord –

Ok- it just wont work! We must speak the word.

I want to encourage you to read the word for yourself.

I'm what you call Holy hood that means half and half the

Hood people say I'm Holy and the Holy people say I'm

hood, it's almost like there's no lane for me.

How many of you remember the Telly

Tubbies a children's Tv show, they use to say "no place

to sit" that is how I felt for a long time. I felt like I didn't

fit in. I didn't go to bible school, but yet I had an

encounter with God and he was qualifying me. The

purpose of me sharing this with you is so you can

understand God loves you and desires a relationship

with you no matter what you have done or been threw. I

am proof that Gods love heals every issue.

I'm excited to share with you that me and my

Father now Pray together no more issues, All is well!

God hasn't done anything for me that he wont do for you. So I want to encourage you. Talk to God yes talk to him just like you would kick it with your friends invite God in your heart. All God needs is your whole heart, check out what the Bible says - Jeremiah 29:13 "You will seek me and find me ,when you seek me with all your heart". Every testimony in here is based off of me seeking God with my whole heart. God guided me and wants to guide you if anyone has ever offended you and you can still replay the moment I want to pray for you.

Father in the name of Jesus I pray that you will touch the person who is reading this I ask you God to bless them and guide them in how to let go of all past hurt, offenses and forgiveness Lord allow them to have eyes to see and ears to hear, and remove any type of denial God. God allow them to remember those who they need to apologies to. I come against the spirit of offense and command it to go now in the name of Jesus. I speak life over you, today you are walking in a new understanding and God forgives you so therefore you forgive others.

Father you are able to do all things I ask by the time they close this book that you would supernatural operate on our heart, create in me a clean heart and renew the right spirit with in me. I want to be what you called me to be. Remove anything that is hindering stopping or blocking me from your plan for my life. I want to walk in the greater today, Lord today I ask you to forgive me for blaming you for all my pain, I thank you God that all things do work together for my good, and you never put more on me then I can bear, thank you for getting me out of situations that should have killed me. You are a good Father. I ask for your forgiveness for the times I was mad at you because of others I repent for closing you out, I invite you into my heart again, and I bless you lord for never leaving me even when I was at my worst you saw the best in me. Lord I ask that you change me and make me more like you. I want your promises, I want you to be my Father I want to feel the love that I have been seeking in other places fill every empty space, I want to know you God so my identity can be fully revealed and I may be whole and healed Thank you Daddy I have no more issues in Jesus name Amen.

DADDY ISSUES

Titanya Verdun Johnson

Made in the USA
Columbia, SC
15 June 2019